My Allah Teaches Me

Introducing Your Muslim Babies to Allah

By The Sincere Seeker Kids Collection

Allah is One.
He is my God.
He created me and
gifted me life.

Allah created the dark nights, the fluffy clouds, the shiny stars, and the bright, sparkly moon.

Allah created the day, the bright blue skies, the colorful rainbow, and the warm yellow sun.

Allah created
the rough,
bumpy
mountains.

Allah created the
deep dark oceans
and colorful sea
creatures.

Allah created tall
green trees,
different colored
plants, and delicate
flowers.

Allah created small animals like fuzzy, soft bunnies and tiny, squeaky hamsters.

Allah created big
animals like big
brown bears and
tall, long-necked
giraffes.

Allah created animals that fly like eagles, falcons, ravens, and hawks that soar high in the sky.

Allah created me,
my parents, my
brother and sister,
and my friends too!

Allah sees everything.
He hears everything.
He is always with me.
He is always watching
over my family and me.

Allah takes care of my family and me. Allah gifted us a warm cozy home and a car that takes us to both distant and close places.

Allah gifts me food to eat like fresh, sweet fruits, juicy chicken, and creamy cheese to stay healthy and strong.

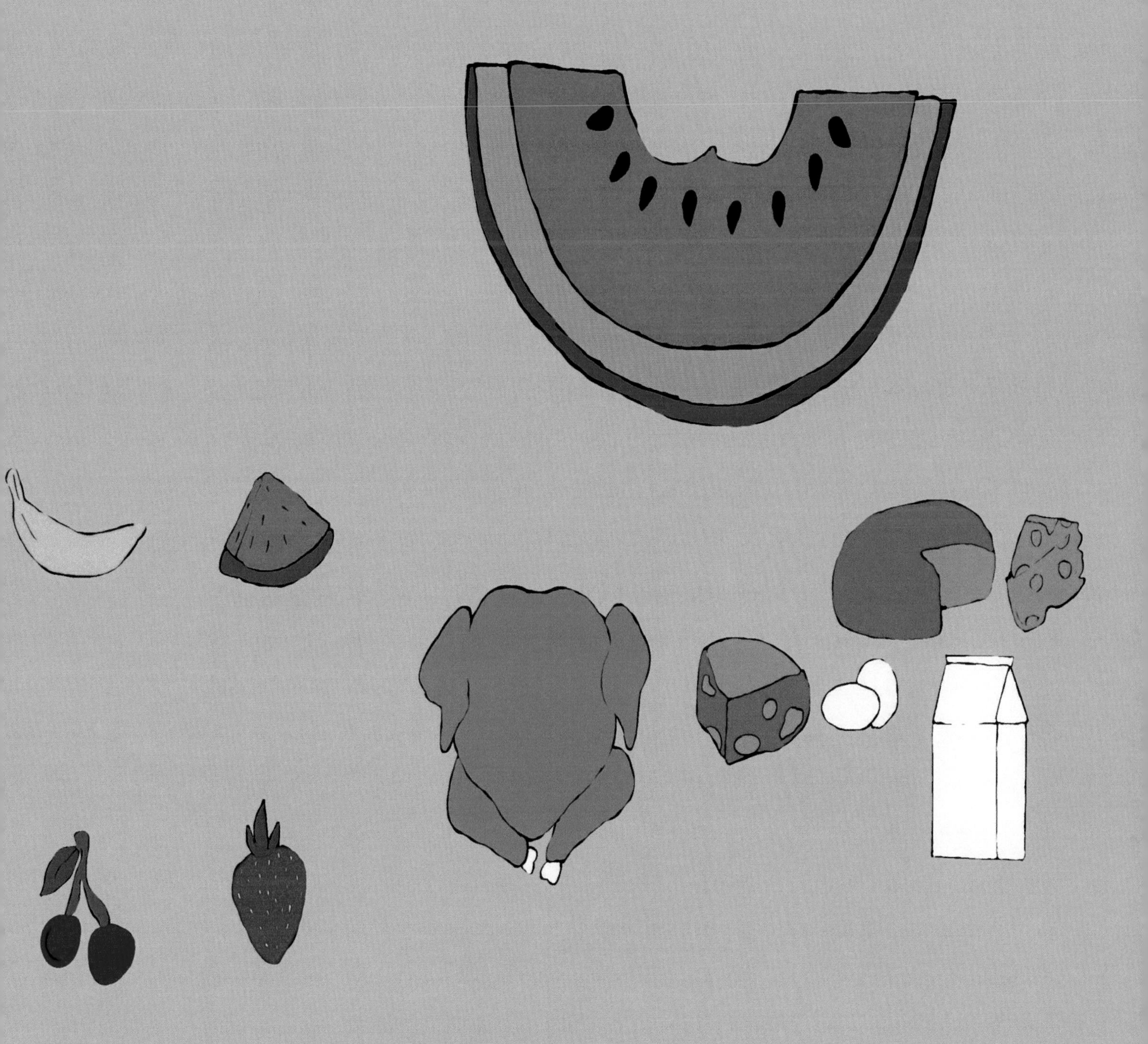

Allah gives me drinks
to quench my thirst.
He gifts me water,
apple juice, and sweet
lemonade on a hot day!

Allah loves my
family and me. And
we love Him too.
Allah keeps us safe
and sound.

Allah gifts me fun toys to play with. Allah gifted my big brother a race car and a doll for my little sister.

Allah gave me hands so I can do things, feet to walk, eyes to see, ears to hear, a nose to smell, a mouth to speak, and a stomach, heart, and brain!

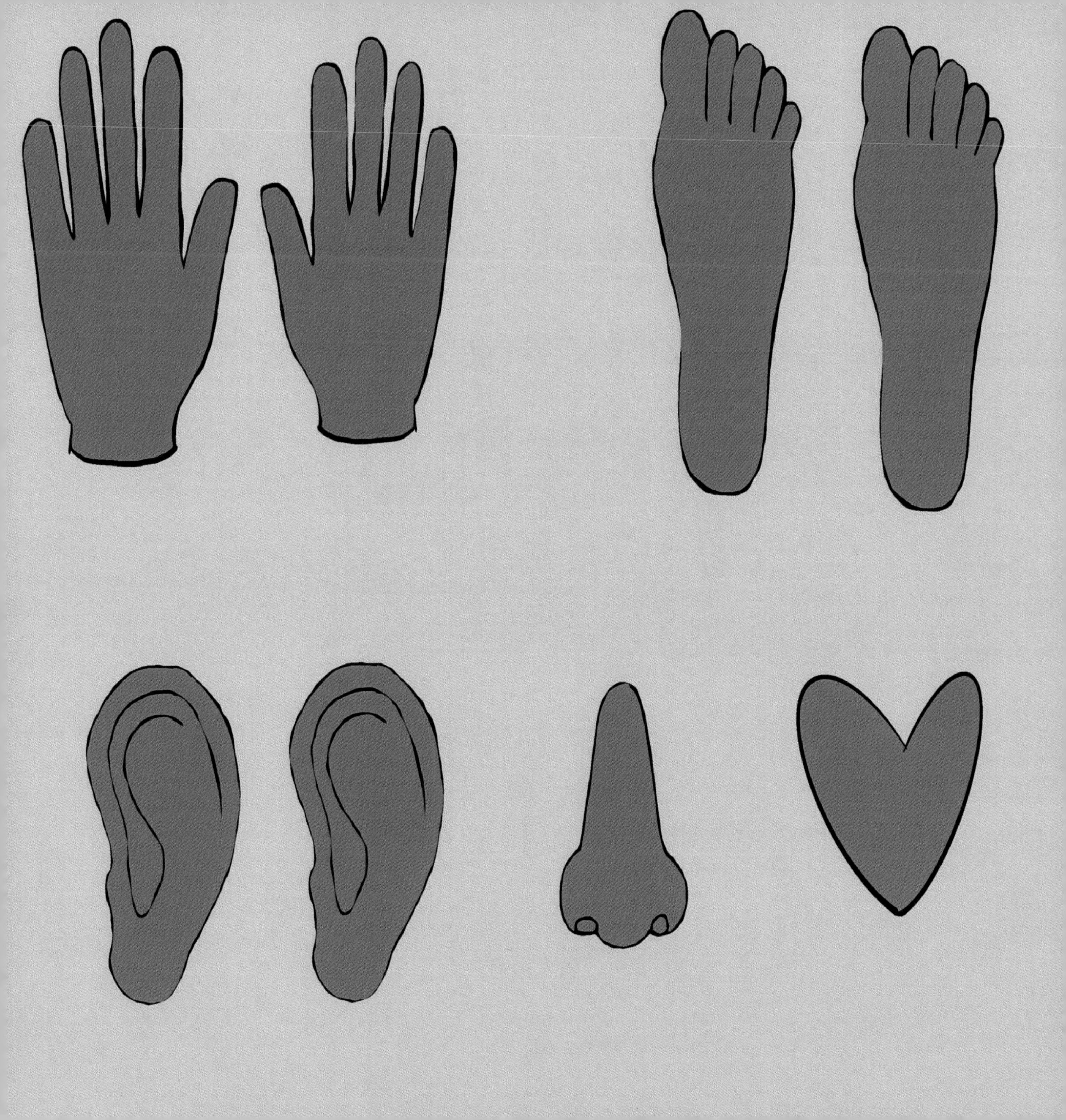

Allah teaches me to be
good to my parents,
brothers, and sisters
to everyone every day!

The Holy Quran is Allah's Word. My parents read Allah's word every day. My parents read pieces of the Holy Quran when they pray too.

Allah gave us a way of
life to live called Islam.
Islam is Allah's religion.

اسلام

My parents pray to Allah every day, asking Him to protect our family and me. He's always listening. I will start to talk and pray to Allah too...

The End.

Made in United States
North Haven, CT
21 April 2023